smart girl's GUIDE

LIKING HERSELF

—even on the bad days

the secrets to trusting yourself,
being your best & never letting
the bad days bring you down

by Dr. Laurie Zelinger
illustrated by Jennifer Kalis

★ American Girl®

Published by American Girl Publishing

18 19 20 21 22 23 24 QP 12 11 10 9 8 7 6 5 4 3

Editorial Development: Carrie Anton
Art Direction and Design: Camela Decaire
Production: Jeannette Bailey, Sarah Boecher, Caryl Boyer,
Tami Kepler, Judith Lary, Kristi Lively, Cynthia Stiles
Illustrations: Jennifer Kalis

Special thanks to: Dr. Fred Zelinger, Dr. Jerry Weisfogel,
Sarah Derene, Jessica Buzel

americangirl.com/service

Dear Reader,

Growing up can be hard. Lots of things keep changing in your life: your body, your family, your school, and your friends. One day everything may feel perfect, and the next day it feels as if things couldn't get any worse.

Those are the bad days. They happen to everyone—yes, everyone! And while there may be no way to escape bad days, it's important to remember that sometimes the difference between a bad day and a terrible day just depends on what you think of yourself. It's called your self-esteem.

When your self-esteem is high, it can make a good day seem even better and a terrible day not as bad. But when your self-esteem is low, it can make a good day not so good and a bad day even worse.

In this book, you'll learn the difference between high and low self-esteem and figure out where you stand. You'll find ways to boost your self-esteem if it's low and ways to keep it pumped up so that it doesn't dip in the future. With the tips in this book, you'll be on your way to being the best you can be, so that you always like yourself a lot—even on bad days.

Your friends at American Girl

contents

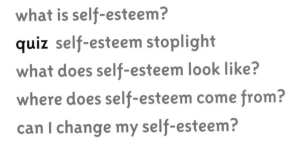

self-esteem: the basics

what is self-esteem?

Self-esteem is a feeling. It's the opinion you have about yourself. Some people call it self-image, self-concept, or self-confidence. Whatever it's called, **it's all about how much you like who you are.**

Self-esteem is not something that you can see on an X-ray or find out about from a blood test. It's not a special place in your body that a doctor can feel or listen to when she examines you. **Your self-esteem is part of you, but it's not an actual body part.** It's the big idea you have about yourself that you carry with you in your heart and in your head.

Your self-esteem is like a little voice that says:

Give it a try!

You're terrific!

Maybe you'll be able to do it, because you've done hard things before! But if you can't, it's no big deal—you can always try again another time.

When your self-esteem is high, you *know* you can do all kinds of things. When your self-esteem is low, you *think* you can't. If you like yourself a lot, you probably have high self-esteem and a good self-image. But if you always find things wrong with yourself, you might have low self-esteem and decide new things aren't even worth trying.

self-esteem stoplight

Take this quiz and see what lights up on your self-esteem traffic light.

1. As you head to the cafeteria for lunch, you think,

a. *I really hope someone will sit by me today so that I don't have to eat alone again.*

b. *I like eating with Amanda, but sometimes I wish we could sit at a more crowded table.*

c. *I can hardly wait until lunch so that I can hang out with my friends. They're saving me a seat.*

2. You think your new haircut looks horrible. Before school, you . . .

a. pretend you're sick so that you can stay home and hide.

b. pack a hat in your backpack and start counting down the days until your next haircut.

c. accessorize your hair with a headband and make the best of it. After all, working with a new style takes some practice.

3. You walk into school and one of the popular girls says, "I like your owl shirt!" You . . .

a. decide she is just being sarcastic.

b. respond, "Who? Me?"

c. smile and say, "Thanks! Isn't it a hoot?"

4. Soccer tryouts are coming up. You decide that you'll . . .

   a. never make the team, so there's no point in trying out.

   b. try out in hopes that the coach will put you in any position, even though you secretly have always wanted to play goalie.

   c. start practicing at home with your sister. Your skills need work, but you'd never forgive yourself if you didn't at least try.

5. The class bully tells you to move your books from "her spot." You . . .

   a. move your stuff faster than the speed of light.

   b. roll your eyes in annoyance at her but then move your books to avoid starting any trouble.

   c. keep your books where they are and politely remind her that you were there first.

6. It's Friday afternoon and you're thinking about the weekend. You . . .

   a. decide that since no one has asked you to do anything, you'll just hang out by yourself.

   b. watch TV and decide you'll head outside if you see the girl next door playing in her yard.

   c. invite the new girl on the block over for pizza and a movie with you and your sister.

Answers

Red Light

If you answered **mostly a's,** your low self-esteem is stopping you from being your best. You feel stuck all by yourself, which makes it easy to envy those around you who are having tons of fun. Even though your confidence needs a jump start, there's still hope! With a little work, you'll soon be traveling down the road toward becoming the person you have always wanted to be.

Yellow Light

If you answered **mostly b's,** your shaky self-esteem has you putting on the brakes. You know what you want, but you don't always have the guts to go after it. Instead of standing strong and stating your opinion, you tend to follow the leader and blend in with traffic. Sure, it's good to compromise sometimes, but if you don't share what you really think, you won't feel confident enough to speed ahead.

Green Light

If you answered **mostly c's,** you're ready to go! Your batteries are charged up with confidence and high self-esteem. You think for yourself and stand up for what you believe in. Even though you're usually sure of yourself, beware of times when you're caught off guard and need some reminders to get back on the high self-esteem track.

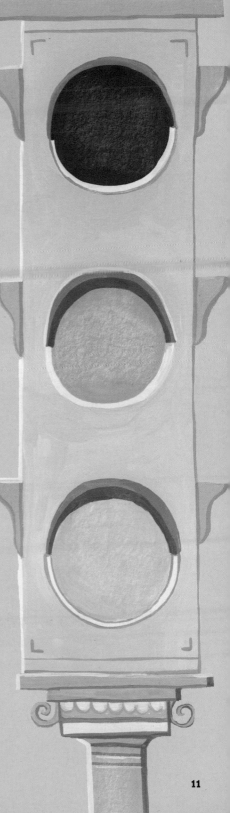

what does self-esteem look like?

Even though your self-esteem is something inside you, the world can see it through your body language. In most situations, a person with high self-esteem looks confident and takes pride in the things she does. That may mean that she stands up straight, walks with her head up and shoulders back, makes eye contact when talking and listening to people, smiles, and appears comfortable in most situations.

Head held high

Smiling

Full face showing

Shoulders relaxed

Back straight

Standing strong

High Self-Esteem

On the flip side, a person with low self-esteem may seem like a droopy puppet hanging from loose strings. Her head and shoulders hang down, and she has trouble looking people in the eyes. She sometimes appears as if she wants to hide from the rest of the world.

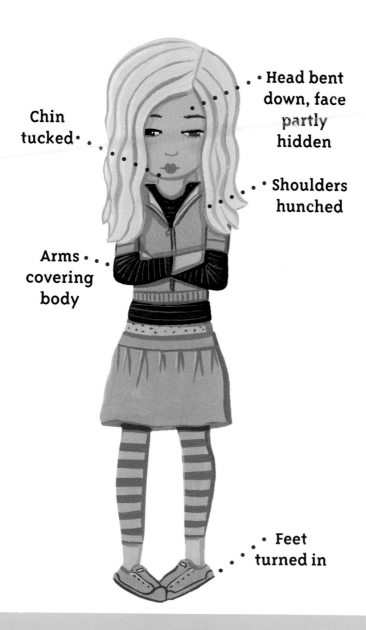

Chin tucked

Head bent down, face partly hidden

Shoulders hunched

Arms covering body

Feet turned in

Low Self-Esteem

where does self-esteem come from?

The simple answer is that your self-esteem comes from within you. But it's really more complicated than that.

Your self-esteem has been building since you were a baby. It comes from all the things that have happened to you as you've grown. As you get older, your self-esteem continues to grow with you, changing with each new experience. Although much of your self-esteem is formed from experiences with others, such as family, teachers, and friends, in the end, it is your responsibility. How you take care of yourself, the choices you make, and the goals you set all play a big part in determining your self-esteem.

Whenever you try something new or hard, you are improving your self-esteem, whether or not you succeed. And if you do this new thing well, your self-esteem takes another step up. The bottom line: You just have to keep trying!

can I change my self-esteem?

Absolutely! Think of yourself as an artist and your self-esteem as a ball of clay that you can shape into anything you choose. It's within your power to sculpt it into exactly what you want it to be. Your first step to doing that is to treat yourself with respect and dignity. Here's how:

Make smart choices. As your parents give you more freedom to do things on your own, they want to know that you will take care of yourself even when they're not around. That means you have to remember the rules and make the kinds of choices for yourself that your parents would likely make for you.

Stay safe. While you and your friends may have lots of cool ideas, you need to steer clear of risky situations in real life and on the Internet. If you think something might go wrong with a plan you have, come up with a new idea.

Don't call yourself names. You've heard the old phrase, "Sticks and stones may break my bones, but words will never hurt me." Well, it's not true. Words can be very hurtful and hard to forget. When other people use words to hurt us, we call them bullies. Don't be a bully by saying mean things to yourself.

Take care of your body. When you're sick, you know how hard—even impossible!—it is to be your best. You may not be able to avoid getting sick, but being good to your body can help you feel better. Stay healthy by getting enough sleep, eating fresh foods, not skipping meals, and getting plenty of exercise.

Show the world your best you. Your self-esteem takes a hit when you don't feel or look your best. Show pride in your appearance with these tips.

- Bathe regularly (at least every other day), and brush your teeth every morning and every night.

- Choose an outfit for the day that is clean. Your clothes don't have to be new or the latest trends, but if they smell like your sneakers, it's time to do some laundry.

- Keep your nails and hands clean. Cut or file your fingernails and toenails weekly, clean dirt from underneath them, and always wash your hands after using the bathroom and before you eat.

Be proud. When you leave the house, walk like a queen wearing a beautiful crown. Stand tall and let the world see the great person that you are—**because you are great!**

Nobody else has done everything that you've done, has lived a life exactly like yours, or is turning out just like you. You are one of a kind. You are unique!

You!

hardworking
thoughtful
creative
caring
funny
responsible
You
You

it's all
about you...

once upon a time . . .

When you were a baby, you were so cute and tiny. Your parents paid a lot of attention to you and took care of everything that you needed. Life was pretty easy for you then.

Then you learned to crawl. You could decide where you wanted to go and could even reach for some things by yourself.

You started to separate from your parents and make friends away from home. You were learning to make your own choices and figuring out what you liked and didn't like.

Your day was filled with lots of learning and responsibility. Besides schoolwork, you were also figuring out things about other kids—such as who was smart or who got into trouble. And those kids were learning about you, too!

Now it's sometimes hard to figure out where you belong and which kids to hang out with. You may try out a few groups before you decide where you feel comfortable.

Your body is changing, and you're not used to it. You knew it would happen one day, but so much is going on that you feel a little confused. Everyone wishes that she could wave a magic wand and choose for herself just how and when her body changes, but that's not the way it works. These physical changes just happen automatically, no matter what you wish for.

you've changed—and that's a good thing!

You might feel self-conscious about the outward changes. But even though you're getting taller and your body is starting to look more grown-up, exciting things are happening inside, too! You're getting better at skills that were once hard for you. You're aware of things you hadn't noticed before, and you care about different things. That's the way it's supposed to be!

Change may seem scary, but without it you'd still be a tiny baby being taken care of by your parents. Some days that may sound great, but what about all the cool things you've done so far that you'd miss out on?

In the space below, list the things that are great about being who you are now:

emotions change, too

Your brain and hormones are sending your body signals to grow in special ways, which might make you feel different than you've felt before. It's important to recognize what you're feeling and learn how to understand or change your emotions when you need to.

Sad: You're down in the dumps and don't see a quick way to feel better. Your eyes are teary, and you feel too tired to smile at things you usually think are funny.

Angry: You have so much energy inside that you feel like yelling or squeezing something. It could even feel like you might explode. Usually this feeling comes when something happens that you think shouldn't have happened.

Worried: You're scared and nervous that something bad is about to happen, and you can't get the idea out of your head. You might have a headache or stomach ache. Another word for this feeling is *anxious*.

Paranoid: You keep expecting something bad to happen and spend all your time watching for signs that it is coming. Even when everything is OK, you think you see clues that things are going to be bad, so you are always on your guard.

Embarrassed: You feel as if everyone is looking and laughing at you for something you did wrong. Your face might turn red and hot and your body might get sweaty. You wish you could snap your fingers and disappear.

Exaggerating the truth

Even the happiest and most self-confident people feel negative emotions once in a while. **Being sad, angry, worried, paranoid, or embarrassed is simply part of life.** However, when your self-esteem is low, these emotions may occur more often, possibly causing you to say mean things to yourself. Doctors who know about behavior call this **distortion,** which means that your mind exaggerates the facts and makes a situation seem worse than it is. It's like looking at something with a **magnifying glass—**everything looks big when it's actually really small.

Distortion happens when something doesn't seem to make sense. For example, if you don't like your hair because you think it's frizzy and then a classmate says she wishes she had hair just like yours, you might not think it is true or think she is being sarcastic. Your brain wants only information that matches the way you already feel. If it doesn't match, your brain has to figure out the truth. If your self-esteem is really low, your brain will distort what your classmate said and find a way to make her words seem like a lie, so that it fits the bad image you already have of yourself.

If you want to **boost your self-esteem,** then you must convince your brain that what the girl said is really true. When you challenge a distortion enough times, it goes away and you see the facts through a normal lens.

It's really a mind game. When your self-esteem is low, your old way of thinking keeps winning because your brain wants to keep things as they are. But with some practice in fighting that distortion, your **good self-image can take the lead.**

Brain games

Think of your brain messages as if they are TV shows: One show features laughter and smiling people, and another is full of insults and mean people. If you want to feel happy, which show would you watch? The first one, of course! It's the same with your self-talk. The messages you play in your brain affect how you feel. If you fill up on positive thoughts, you'll more likely **feel positive about yourself.** But stock up on negative talk, and you're probably not going to feel great about yourself.

Brain A:
So you have a zit on your face. No sweat. Everyone gets them. With the great hair day you're having and the new sweater you wearing, no one will even notice that itty-bitty, teeny-tiny blemish. And if they do, who cares? Make a joke about it. "Anyone for a game of connect the dots?" Laugh it off and move on. People will admire your carefree attitude!

Brain B:
You're so ugly. Just look at that gigantic zit on your face! Everyone is looking right at it. If your mom doesn't let you stay home from school this week, then you'd better think about wearing a paper bag over your head until it goes away. You don't want to scare everyone, do you?

retrain your brain

When your mind goes into magnifying-glass mode and negative self-talk is all you hear, **set your brain straight.**

Step one: It's not what you think

Remember that . . .

- other people really don't look at you as closely as you look at yourself. In fact, they're probably hoping that you don't notice things that they're stressing about.

- almost nothing lasts forever. What people notice or say today may just as quickly be forgotten tomorrow.

- what you're noticing now is only a tiny part of you. All the other parts you like are still there.

- spending less time thinking about bad things leaves more time for fun stuff

- by next week, you'll hardly remember why you had a bad day today.

Step two: Change the channel

If you don't like feeling down in the dumps, change the channel in your mind. Doing something different can help shift your focus from the negatives to the positives.

Here are some ideas.

- Dance to a peppy song.
- Play a board game with your little sister.
- Make a card for your mom.
- Invite a friend over to watch a movie.
- Read a book.
- Clean your room.
- Bake some cookies with your dad.
- Make place cards to put at the table for your next family meal.
- Invent new ways to sign your name.
- Invent a tongue twister you can teach your friends.
- Practice writing with your other hand.
- Memorize the alphabet backward.
- Plant some seeds in an empty egg carton.

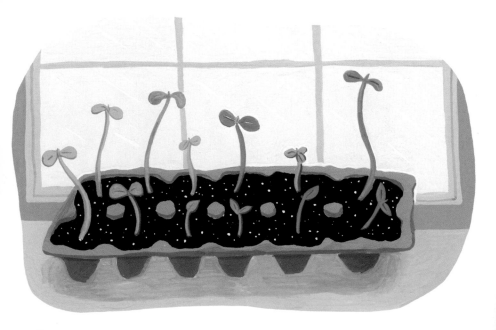

Step three: Look for the positive in yourself

When you feel down about yourself, you forget about **your wonderful qualities.** Use the cootie catcher in the back of the book to learn more about what you *really* think and feel. Punch out the cootie catcher and play it alone or with your friends.

How to play

1. Insert your pointer fingers and thumbs under the numbered flaps.

2. Ask a friend or family member to choose a number from one of the outside flaps. Open and close your fingers that number of times, moving your fingers front to back and then side to side.

3. Have your friend choose a word from the inside of the cootie catcher. Spell out the word, opening and closing your fingers with each letter.

4. Have your friend pick one of the words that shows. Open that flap and read the question beneath it. Have your friend answer the question. Take turns so that you can answer a question, too!

Step four: Look for the positives in others

Thinking positive messages about yourself can help boost your self-esteem, and so can thinking nice things **about the people around you.** Try this challenge. Think of a word that starts with the same sound as each girl's name below. Find a nice word to describe the girl, and put that word in front of her name. For instance, you might say Helpful Hailey, Amazing Abigail, or Marvelous Marley. Try the names below; then make a list of your friends and classmates. What word would go in front of your own name?

_____ Rina

_____ Sofia

_____ Amanda

_____ Brianna

_____ Danielle

_____ Erin

_____ Hannah

_____ Gabriella

_____ Leah

_____ Katie

_____ Paige

_____ Isabel

Step five: Chill out

On some days, **quieting your brain** and putting down the magnifying glass will be harder than on others. On such days, you need to just chill out and be nice to yourself. It can feel good to do something that doesn't take a lot of thought or effort.

- Draw a picture of your family.
- In your journal, record a joke that always makes you laugh.
- Make a rubbing of a leaf by putting it between two pieces of paper. Color over the leaf with a colored pencil, and watch the image come through.
- Rewrite the words to your favorite song.
- Find a magazine story, cross out random words, and fill them in with your class's spelling words.
- Take a bubble bath.
- Have a belly laugh with a friend.
- Take a nap to recharge your batteries.
- Blow up a balloon. With a marker, write things all over it that make you sad, angry, worried, paranoid, and embarrassed. When you're done, pop the balloon. See how little those bad things have become?

Help is on the way

Retraining your brain won't happen overnight, so give it some time. If you've tried and still can't seem to shake negative thoughts, talk to someone about it. Parents, teachers, school psychologists, social workers, school nurses, and guidance counselors are there to help. They are experienced and have most likely helped other kids who've felt like you do. They understand what you're going through and will take what you have to say seriously.

the future factor

When you wonder about who you are and who you want to become, some thoughts are about the near future: "Will I pass the social studies quiz?" "What sport should I try out for next season?" "What dress should I wear to the school dance?" And some thoughts are about the distant future: "Will I go to college?" "What kind of career will I have when I grow up?" "Will I fall in love with someone?" "Will I travel around the world?"

No matter what you're wondering, thoughts can make you feel all kinds of ways—excited, scared, exhilarated, confused, and overwhelmed, to name a few. Life can be like riding a roller coaster. There are ups and downs, fast and slow parts, bumps and shaky parts, and even times when you're thrown for a loop. You can't control which way the track (or in this case, life events) will take you. When you're at the bottom, you can see only what's right in front of you, but when you get to the top, you can see the whole picture a lot better. When you're starting out, accept how you feel and try to enjoy the ride. When it's over, you'll see that it was really cool—even if you couldn't see that when you first started.

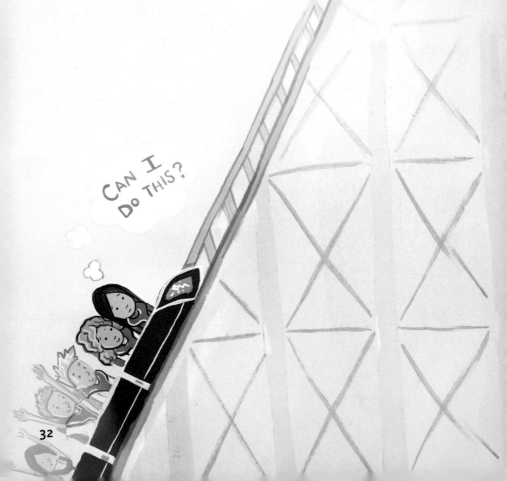

Make a life-changing moment happen by doing something courageous for the first time ever. Challenge yourself!

is shyness stopping you?

How does it feel to watch from the sidelines? Would you rather be part of the action, or do you feel fine about being a spectator? If you really want to join in the fun but something is holding you back, it could be low self-esteem. It could also be that you're just shy.

The shy type

When you're shy, you're more of a watcher than a doer. Shy girls often speak in a soft voice and have trouble making eye contact in conversations. They are quiet and usually have a few close friends whom they feel comfortable with.

Shyness vs. low self-esteem—what's the difference?

There are similarities between being shy and having low self-esteem. Girls in both groups most likely . . .

- are quiet.
- avoid being the center of attention.
- get nervous, scared, or embarrassed around large groups of people.

But here's where the likeness ends: A shy girl typically doesn't mind watching rather than doing. But a girl with low self-esteem does mind. She would like to be the center of attention once in a while but hasn't built up the courage to try just yet. It doesn't mean she can't ever do it; it's more that her self-esteem needs a boost before she'll be brave enough to put herself out there.

are you the shy type?

Low self-esteem or just plain shy? Take our quick quiz to see.

1. At recess, a spontaneous game of kickball—your absolute fave!—breaks out. But instead of getting on the field to pitch the big red ball, you decide to watch. You think:

  a. *I'm nervous about asking everyone if I can join in.*

  b. *I'm sure I'll just trip over my own feet running to second base. I'd rather watch than live through that nightmare.*

  c. *There are too many players already. I'll cheer this time and see if I can jump in on the next game.*

2. Your mom says it's time for you to get a haircut. She asks if you want to get just a trim or if you want your hair shorter, like your favorite actress's hairstyle. You stick with a trim. You think:

  a. *A new haircut would draw more attention to me than I'd like. I prefer to blend in.*

  b. *Stephanie, the popular girl, got her hair cut last week. Everyone will think I'm copying her if I get a new style, too.*

  c. *My favorite actress has beautiful wavy hair, but my hair is super straight. I think the style I have looks great on me and works better with my hair type.*

3. For the next reading project, your teacher lets you decide between doing a written report or an oral presentation. You choose the written report. You think:

a. *Speaking in front of the class makes my palms sweat and my heart race and gives me a stomach ache.*

b. *My retainer makes me slur my words. I don't need to be known for the rest of the semester as "Little Miss Lisp."*

c. *I've done a few oral reports for other subjects and need a break. I love writing and am really good at it, so this project will be fun!*

4. At the school-play kickoff meeting, you're told to stand on the left side of the room if you want to try out for the cast and on the right side if you want to have a guaranteed spot on the crew. You stand on the right side of the room. You think:

a. *My knees shake just imagining all those eyes staring at me as I sing.*

b. *I'll forget my lines onstage, ruining the play for sure.*

c. *I love art and I've always wanted to make stage props. Now's the perfect chance to try it!*

Answers

Break out of your shell

If you answered **mostly a's,** you're the shy and quiet type. Your self-esteem may need a little lift, but not necessarily. Shyness doesn't mean that you have low self-esteem. Check in with yourself to see how you're feeling. If you're happy with standing on the sidelines and have good reasons for keeping to yourself, then your shyness is likely not a problem. However, if your shyness stops you from doing things that you want to do, then reconsider your actions. Confident people can be quiet, but they aren't afraid to try new experiences. Everything you ever learned to do was once brand-new. And you did it. So go for it!

Look for the positive in you

If you answered **mostly b's,** your confidence needs a boost. No one is good at everything, so you can't expect that from yourself. Instead of worrying about all the things you can't do right or that could go wrong, focus on what you do well. The more often you remind yourself that you have skills that other people don't have, the stronger you'll feel inside. If you believe in yourself, that confidence will give you the courage to try new things. Before you know it, you'll be great at those new things, too!

Stay on your healthy course

If you answered **mostly c's,** you're comfortable with yourself as you are. You make decisions based on your likes and dislikes instead of on what others will think of you or how you will be judged. You're willing to take risks and try new things. Not everything will work out perfectly, but you know that nothing is perfect. All you can do is try your best.

yikes!

Everyone has had an embarrassing moment. If you've suffered through one, you know how it feels—the red cheeks, the wave of heat, the strong wish to have the floor swallow you up right where you're standing. The lesson is to not get hung up on it but to just let it roll off you so that you can get back to feeling "normal." Girls just like you have done it, and so can you!

We were having spirit week at school, and one of the days was "dress like a pirate" day. I forgot that spirit week started on Tuesday. I showed up dressed like a pirate—on Monday! So all day I said to everyone, "I'm a pirate! Arrr!" Everybody laughed, and it turned out to be pretty fun.

—Lindsay C.

Age 12, Maryland

My mom and I were sitting on a beach. Suddenly there was a big wave, and tons of sand and water sprayed us. We had to walk back to the house soaking wet with sand in our hair. We looked really funny!

—Kei T.

Age 11, New York

I was at the lake and saw a cool fish swimming in the water. I leaned over to look at it, and before I knew it, I was soaked from head to toe! My family laughed at me. I have to admit that if I had seen myself fall in the water, I would have laughed, too!

—Katie C.
Age 11, Maryland

One time during social studies, I was leaning back in my chair. Suddenly I fell backward with a very loud BANG! Everyone in my class just looked at me lying there on the floor. I recovered by laughing along with everyone else.

Shelby B.
Age 13, New Jersey

Once at school, I wore a white skirt. It had rained, but I forgot and went down a slide. I got a *huge* wet spot on my skirt. I had to tie a friend's coat around my waist for the rest of the day.

—Elizabeth B.
Age 13, Alabama

One summer, my family and I went for a walk outside. I was walking ahead of them when, all of a sudden, a huge turkey jumped out in front of me! It chased me all the way down a hill. We still laugh about it today.

—Ashley R.
Age 13, Ohio

i can!

Improving your self-esteem happens one step at a time. For a quick boost, start replacing the words "I can't" with "I can."

Start with something small. Goals that are just a little out of your reach are easier to accomplish and make you feel successful when you achieve them. Make a list of things you've always wanted to try, or go for one of the following:

• **Memorize** the names of your distant relatives.

• **Learn** how to say a phrase in a foreign language.

• **Dare** yourself to finish a project before it is due.

• **Eat** an extra serving of vegetables every day for a week.

• **Read** for an extra half hour every day.

When you push yourself beyond your comfort zone, your brain will send you cheers for trying. Accomplish something small at first, and you'll have the confidence to go bigger next time.

self-esteem starts at home

Even when you're old enough to do things for yourself, your family is still an important support to you as you become the strong person you want to be.

The perfect audience

It takes courage to try new things, and trying them in front of strangers can feel even more scary. Before you step in front of a crowd of people you barely know, let your family be your own mini audience. If you've always wanted to . . .

sing in a choir,
TRY singing along with the radio while you and your mom do dishes.

dance on the school jazz team,
TRY making up a dance routine for you and your sister to do together.

act in a community play,
TRY memorizing a poem to recite during dinner.

join gymnastics,
TRY stretching with your dad before his morning run. He can loosen his hamstrings while you master your splits.

share a homemade treat in class,
TRY making brownies to serve for dessert this weekend.

go out for the basketball team,
TRY shooting rolled socks into the laundry basket with your big brother.

be in a school spelling bee,
TRY playing a word-themed board game with your whole family.

Be open to feedback—but don't take it the wrong way!

Using your family as an audience can help you feel comfortable doing a new activity in front of other people, and it's also a great way to get instant feedback and tips to help you improve. Sometimes, however, feedback can be taken the wrong way. For example:

Feedback given:

> **These brownies are yummy! You should make another batch using peanut butter chips instead of chocolate chips and take them over to Grandma and Grandpa's house.**

What you heard:

> **I liked the brownies, but they would've been better if you'd made them differently.**

A suggestion—which may sound like criticism to you—can be hard to hear, but when it comes from someone who loves and supports you, it's not supposed to feel bad. It's just another idea for you to think about. **Your family wants to help you do your best,** and the tips they give you are meant to help you, not hurt you. Because they spend so much time with you and know you better than anyone, you can count on honest feedback, honest answers, and full support.

Ask questions

Family members can answer questions you might be too embarrassed to ask anyone else. They can tell you what it's like to jump off a diving board, to be at the top of a snow-covered ski mountain, or to sleep away from home for the first time. When you want to do something for the first time but are afraid, your family can give you the encouragement you need to try.

new expectations

Just as you can count on your parents to help you develop new skills
and talents that interest you, your parents are going to start counting on
you to help out around the house more, be responsible for yourself, and
make good choices without them. Compared to when you were little,
house rules may change.

When you were little . . .	Now . . .
you'd play all day.	you do homework, play one hour of computer games, and watch 30 minutes of TV.
your parents would feed you veggies.	you help prepare the veggies.
you'd throw dirty clothes into the hamper.	you fold laundry and put it away.
your parents scheduled playdates for you.	you are trusted to go to a friend's house and come home when told.
you'd play nicely with your siblings.	you babysit for your siblings.

Let's face it: Chores, homework, and keeping track of your busy schedule
aren't as easy as playing all day, but as you master these new responsibilities, you're showing your parents that you're ready to have freedom and
you're OK when they can't be with you.

Rewarding responsibilities

Don't think of your new responsibilities as burdens. Instead, think of how you can let your self-esteem shine—and of the payoffs that could result!

Keep your room neat, pick up your clothes from the floor, and make your bed without being asked, and maybe . . . your parents will let you redecorate your space in the aqua blue surf theme you've been dreaming about.

Do your homework on time, keep up your grades, and spend free time reading instead of watching TV, and maybe . . . your parents will surprise you with the e-reader you wanted for your next birthday.

Regularly babysit for your little brother while your parents run errands on Saturday mornings, and maybe . . . your parents will see that you are responsible enough to take care of the kitten you've always wanted.

Turn off the lights and TV when you leave a room, put dirty dishes into the dishwasher, and follow house rules regarding lights-out at night, and maybe . . . your parents will let you have the slumber party you've been begging to throw.

Remind your mom early about your school events, such as the talent show, the fund-raising rummage sale, and the 40 cupcakes you need for a class party, and maybe . . . your parents will let you take the Thursday-night crochet class at the local craft store.

talking to parents

You used to want to spend every minute with your parents and tell them every little thing about your day. **Now you're more comfortable talking to and hanging out with your friends,** and being around your parents isn't as cool as it used to be. What happened?

When you're worried about what other people think of you, being seen with your parents can feel like embarrassing torture. And as you're going through all kinds of changes, you might think that your family will see you as some sort of weirdo. You'd still like to talk to your parents about plenty of things, but you have no idea how they'll react. You don't even know how to start the conversation.

First, remember that your parents were your age once—*yes, really!* Visualizing that might make it easier to open up to them.

Next, find a time when one of them isn't so busy.

Good times to try:
• In the car
• While eating dinner
• During TV time together
• While folding laundry
• Before bedtime

Times to avoid:
• In the morning when everyone is trying to get out the door for school and work
• As soon as your parents walk in the door from work. Give your mom some time to get her coat and shoes off and to settle down a little.
• While your parents are busy paying the bills or on the phone

When face-to-face is too much
Can't get the words to come out? Try . . .
• writing a note and leaving it on their bed or bathroom mirror.
• sending your dad a text message—even if he's just in the next room.
• leaving a voicemail for one of them to listen to at work.

Icebreakers

Now comes the hard part—what to say. Try one of these questions to get the conversation started:

May I talk to you about something?

You know what I've been thinking about lately?

Mom, did you ever worry about stuff when you were a kid?

What did you and your friends talk about when you were my age?

What kinds of places did Grandma and Grandpa let you go to alone when you were young?

Did you ever have a diary? What did you write in it?

Is it normal to feel . . . ?

Your parents will most likely figure out that you're trying to bring up a tricky topic and will help you get the words out. They want to know what's going on in your life and what you've been up to, but they probably don't want to pry. So even if your cheeks turn bright red and your heart races, your parents will be glad you came to them to talk.

friendship ties

"A friend accepts us as we are yet helps us to be what we should." Author unknown

Just as your family can help boost your self-esteem, so can your friends. A good friend can help you feel strong and will be there when you need a shoulder to cry on, a good laugh, a big hug, or someone by your side when you try something new.

You might have best friends, camp friends, school friends, team friends, neighborhood friends, old friends, new friends, and maybe even faraway friends. There are also kids in your class who aren't your close friends, but you see them every day and are nice to each other. It's no surprise that your friends are mega important to how you feel about yourself.

great friendships

A friend feels like part of your family and knows you very well. You know she's on your side even when she isn't around. She wants the best for the both of you, remembers what you like, and always cheers you on. She pumps up your confidence and helps you try for the things you want. She wants to be your friend as much as you want to be hers. To keep that friendship special, here are friendship tips you'll need from A to Z!

Acceptance
Love your friends for who they are—even if they have little quirks.

Belly Laughs
These are best shared with friends. Get one started with a silly tongue twister.

Cheering Up
If your friend is feeling blue, make her smile.

Differences
You and your friend won't always agree. If you disagree with something she says, let her know. Say, "That's one way to look at it, but this is how I see it."

Effort
Don't always wait for your friend's invitation. Make sure you call her sometimes and invite her to do something together.

Fun

What's a friendship without a lot of fun?

Gabbing

There's nothing like a good gab with a friend, whether you're chatting in person or on the phone. Just keep the other "G" word—gossip—out of it.

Honesty

Be honest with your friends. If a friend hurts your feelings, tell her. Say, "Remember what happened the other day? I was really hurt by . . ."

Independence

You and your friend love to spend time together, but you should also spend time apart. You'll both have experiences that you can tell each other about the next time you're together.

Jokes

Save a good joke for a time when your friend needs a laugh.

Kindness

The more you give, the more you receive.

Listening

When your friend talks to you, really listen to her. If you are thinking about what you are going to say next, you aren't really paying attention.

Manners

Even though you are with her a lot, don't forget to say "please" and "thank you" to your friend.

Nicknames

Having special names for each other is like having your own friendship code.

Oops!

No friendship is perfect. Say "I'm sorry" when you may have hurt your friend.

Pictures

Photos capture great memories. Bring a camera on your next fun get-together.

Questions

Asking questions to get to know your friend better is OK, but don't ask any that will embarrass her.

Reliability

If you promise to spend Saturday afternoon with your friend, follow through. She'll know you're true-blue.

Sharing
Friends share everything from clothes to books. Give a due date when you want an item returned. If a friend has had something too long, it's OK to ask for it back.

Thoughtfulness
Little things mean a lot. The next time your friend is home sick, take extra-good notes about homework assignments for her.

Understanding
Be understanding when she makes a mistake.

Variety
Try new things together. Make a list of fun things you want to do, and check them off as you do them.

Wishes
Make a wish on a shooting star for your friend.

XOXO
Next time you send her a text, don't forget a sweet sign-off, such as XOXO. Or make up one of your own, such as SYLS (See You Later, Sunshine) or LWYL (Laugh With Ya Later).

Yes!
Encourage each other in everything you both do. Go to one of your friend's games just to cheer her on.

ZZZ
ZZZ stands for sleepover! Get your gal pals together and have one to celebrate your friendship.

how friendly are you?

Do you actively look for new friends, or do you hope friends find their way to you? Take this quiz and find out.

1. Think of the last time you and a friend did something fun together. How did you make the plans?

　a. My friend called me and invited me.

　b. I asked my mom to call my friend's mom to figure it out.

　c. I called my friend and invited her.

2. Lucky you! Mom said you can have a summer sleepover. Who's coming?

　a. Just my best friend. Keeping it small is more fun.

　b. My three BFFs. We've been friends since first grade.

　c. A few old friends, a couple of newer friends, and a girl I met at day camp last week.

3. You're at the ice cream shop, and you see that girl who just moved to your neighborhood. What do you do?

　a. I sneak a peek at her and keep licking the drips on my ice cream cone.

　b. I smile and give her a little wave.

　c. I say, "Yum, I love mint chip, too!" and introduce myself.

4. Your family is at your mom's company picnic. You don't know anyone there, but you see a bunch of kids playing Frisbee®. What do you do?

a. I hang close to my family and watch the kids from a distance.

b. I wander close to the kids and hope someone misses the Frisbee so that I can grab it and join in.

c. I run up to the kids and say, "Hey, I love Frisbee! Can I play?"

5. Your friend tells you that her cousin is coming for the weekend—all the way from Canada. What do you say?

a. "That's great! You must be excited."

b. "Give me a call if you two go to the movies or something."

c. "I'd love to meet her! Maybe you can both come over and have pizza at my house."

6. *Brrring!* Your sister's friend is on the phone. What do you say?

a. "Just a sec," and then holler for your sis.

b. "Hi. My sister's upstairs on the computer. I'll go get her, but it might take a minute."

c. "Hey, Carly! I was just thinking about you yesterday because I saw a girl who looked just like you at the pool. I waved and everything, but it wasn't you! Yeah, I was embarrassed. I knew you'd laugh when you heard about it, though. Anyway, here's my sister. Talk to you later."

7. You haven't talked to your friend in a while. What do you do?

a. You wonder what you did to upset her.

b. You give her a couple more days and see if she calls.

c. You call her to see what's up.

8. You and your mom are at the bookstore and you run into Mrs. Glick, a woman your mom knows from college. Mrs. Glick comments on the book you're buying and asks how old you are now. What do you say?

a. Nothing. Your mom jumps in and says, "She'll be ten next month."

b. "I'm almost ten."

c. "I'm almost ten, and I can't wait to read this. I've read all the others in the series. Have you?"

Mostly a's

You love the friends you have (which is great), but you're not always sure about meeting new people. Once in a while, get to know someone new. Don't miss the chance to make a friend.

Mostly b's

You're happy just being a bud. You don't worry too much about your friendships. When your friends call, you love to get together. But don't always wait for someone else to make the effort—it's good for you to reach out, too.

Mostly c's

You're a friend finder. Confident and outgoing, you love meeting new people. Be sure to make time for all of your friends—old and new alike.

making friends

Some girls can walk into a room full of strangers and **attract people like a magnet.** When you watch these girls talk, laugh, and play with new people, you'd think they'd known each other all their lives instead of for only a few minutes. But meeting new people isn't easy for everyone.

Hide and seek

Potential friends are everywhere—you just have to know where to look!

- In your neighborhood
- On your bus
- In your camp group
- In your class
- On your sports team
- At your place of worship
- Where you volunteer
- Where you play
- In your family (sisters, brothers, and cousins can be friends, too!)

Start small

If there's someone you'd like to get to know better but don't know how to go about it, try . . .

- sitting next to her at the next activity you do together.
- asking if you can eat lunch at her table.
- complimenting her. Sometimes saying something such as "I like your shoes" can lead to a longer conversation.
- asking if you can join in the game she's playing at recess.
- picking her to be on your team in gym class.
- asking her to be your partner for your next school project.

Be your own friend

If you have a hard time making new friends, **be a friend to yourself first.**

Be yourself. Feel proud of the things that make you who you are—your talents, your style, your interests—and you'll attract people who appreciate you, too.

Don't sell yourself short. Don't stop yourself from meeting someone new because you think she is better than you or wouldn't be interested in the same things you are. Since no two people are alike, a friend doesn't have to be just like you.

Let go of labels. "Cool kids," "popular girls," and "nerds" are just words. Don't let labels define who you are or limit the people you'd like to meet.

Help friends come to you. You don't always have to approach another person to kick things off. Simply being nice to other people makes you more approachable. By smiling and making eye contact, others won't think that you just want to be left alone.

Pick friends who lift you up. You want to fit in, but when you're desperate to be accepted by anyone, you might choose friends who bring you down—kids who get into trouble at school, break rules, or make bad decisions. If you have low self-esteem, you might be attracted to this crowd because you don't feel worthy of better friends. But you're wrong; **you deserve better!** Treat yourself to friends who help you feel your best.

beware of frenemies

Before you can become friends with someone, you have to get to know her a little. Even if you both like all the same things, that doesn't mean that you're going to click as friends. Sometimes things just don't feel right. That's OK. You don't have to force it. **A friend is someone you can be your real self around.** If you don't meet a new friend today, you will another day.

But there are *frenemies*—people who start out as friends but who say or do mean things. You don't always trust a frenemy, but you hang out with her anyway because she's part of your bigger group of friends and you don't want to make waves. And besides, sometimes she's nice, and you never know how she's going to act from one day to the next. Or you simply don't know how to break away from her without creating a lot of drama.

gossip   lies

rumors
                    drama
cliques
              secrets

Be free of frenemies

Friends who appreciate you boost your confidence, whereas frenemies usually bring you down. Hanging out with people who can't be trusted isn't good for you—so it's time to do what's best for you.

Make good choices. If a frenemy tries to get you to do something that you know will get you into trouble, it's best to do the opposite. Do what's right now, and you won't regret it later.

Speak up. If a frenemy says something that hurts your feelings, tell her. It's OK to say, "I don't like it when . . . " Chances are she didn't intend to be mean. But if she did, you don't want her as a friend anyway.

Clear the air. If you once considered a frenemy a real friend, something might have caused her to act differently. Talk with her to see if you can hit the "refresh" button on your friendship. If that doesn't work, it's OK to walk away from a friendship.

Quiz

Can you tell if a friend will be there until the end? Decide if each of the following comments came from a friend or a frenemy.

1. "Tell your mom we're studying, but we'll really go to the movies. She won't find out."

             friend   **frenemy**

2. You're trying a new style, and you ask your friend for advice. She says, "Your new sweater is cute, but it might look better with the jeans you wore last weekend."

             friend   **frenemy**

3. After you've been elected class vice president, you overhear your friend say, "It's a good thing she ran with Brenna as president or she wouldn't have gotten any votes."

             friend   **frenemy**

4. "Even though we're going to Sasha's sleepover on Saturday, let's not ask her to go to the park with us. She's so boring! We can make up an excuse if we run into her."

             friend   **frenemy**

5. The math test is coming up, and you could use a study buddy. You ask your friend, and she says, "I studied for the test last night, but I could meet you at the library after school to go over the problems again."

             friend   **frenemy**

Answers

1. frenemy, 2. friend, 3. frenemy, 4. frenemy, 5. friend

we used to be friends

When you were little, your friends were either children of your parents' friends, your siblings, or children from day care, a play group, or preschool. At that age you mostly played by yourself, alongside other kids your age, so it really didn't matter to you who they were.

As you got older, you began choosing your own friends. **Those friends became special**—you liked playing with them, talking to them, and sharing secrets. They liked spending time with you, too.

If you've been friends a long time, you've most likely seen each other change over the years. That's because just as you are changing every day, your friends are doing the same. And you may **notice changes in your friendships.**

You might not be as close with some of the girls you were friends with before. As your worlds expand, you might develop new friendships with girls from soccer, your scout troup, religious school, and other places where you spend time. As you get older, your interests change, too, which might cause you to grow apart from someone who used to be your best friend.

Growing apart from a friend is different from ending a friendship. You grow apart because different things have become more important in each of your lives, and you now have less in common. You may naturally start spending less time together without any conversation about doing so. It may feel a little awkward at first, but eventually, you find that you've each gone your separate way—with new friends—and you're both fine with seeing each other when you pass in the halls. No hard feelings.

In contrast, when you end a friendship, the break may start with a fight, a misunderstanding, jealousy, or gossip that was spread. Good friends can fight, make up, and get right back to where they were before the fight.

But that's not always the case when feelings are hurt.

Staying friends

True friends trust each other, but fighting and gossip can break that trust. If a friend makes you feel great about yourself, she's probably a keeper. It takes a lot of courage to do, but try to work things out. Here's how:

Talk it out. Just as words can get jumbled in the "telephone game," a misunderstanding or fight can start based on something you heard from a friend, who heard it from a friend, who heard it from a friend. Get the truth directly from the source.

Listen. Everyone has different opinions. You don't have to agree with those opinions, but a good friend will give the other friend a chance to speak her mind.

Say you're sorry. If you know that something you did or said hurt your friend, come clean and apologize.

Rebuild trust. Saying you're sorry doesn't mean much if you turn around and do the hurtful thing again. If you say it, mean it and remember it!

Make things right. Simply saying sorry may help, but your friend may need more help to get over a big fight. Ask her if there is anything you can do to make things right, and then follow through.

Accept apologies. Accepting an apology can be just as hard as giving one. But if things can be fixed, forgiveness is the first step to getting your friendship back to normal.

Taking a break

If you and your friend are fighting more and more, and it's making you feel sad all the time, your friendship probably isn't working out. **It's not healthy to keep bringing out the worst in each other.** It's time for a break.

Ending a friendship is hard to do and may mean a big change for both of you. Talk to your friend about taking a break. Tell her why you think it's not working out, and be polite. Just because you can't be friends anymore doesn't mean you need to be mean to each other. Avoid saying hurtful things or spreading gossip. Figure out a way that you'll both feel better about yourselves by ending the friendship on a positive note.

be your
best

she's so cool

There are all kinds of reasons you admire people, especially the ones who seem to be special in some way. Take this quiz to see what makes you sometimes want to be "just like her."

1. At the spring school assembly, the principal announces that awards and trophies will be given to outstanding students. The cool girl receives . . .

   a. the school spirit award for signing up so many new members for the after-school clubs.

   b. a big trophy for scoring the most goals on this year's school soccer team.

   c. a gigantic dictionary—it's so big that two people have to carry it in!—for winning the school spelling bee.

   d. a 48-piece acrylic paint set for winning the state art contest.

2. When the cool girl walks in, the first thing you notice about her is . . .

   a. how all the other girls run over to her to say hi.

   b. she's still in her cleats and must have come straight from practice.

   c. her saying that she's so happy to be at the party because she's spending the rest of the weekend studying for a science test.

   d. how cool she looks with the different-patterned shirts she's layered on top of one another.

3. The cool girl shows her favorite birthday present to her friends. It's . . .

   a. the same shoes that all of her friends wear in different colors.

   b. a new warm-up suit to wear to and from gymnastics.

   c. a messenger bag with tons of pockets for her school supplies.

   d. a scarf that she knit from the boldly colored yarn she was given.

4. Mr. Davis is the substitute teacher today. You can't believe the cool girl was able to convince him . . .

   a. to let the class work in groups so that everyone can sit with friends.

   b. that it is gym day instead of music day.

   c. to let the class have a study hour during the last period.

   d. to read and discuss her favorite author's poems.

5. It's finally recess time and the doors are open to the playground. The cool girl heads out . . .

   a. to find all her friends in their usual spot.

   b. with a basketball and starts setting up teams.

   c. with her book and reads quietly under the tree.

   d. to make up a dance with another friend.

6. Everyone is encouraged to sign up for one after-school activity. The cool girl . . .

   a. asks her friends what they're taking and goes with them.

   b. asks the gym teacher if she's running any of them.

   c. joins a science-experiments club.

   d. is deciding between jazz band and glee club.

Answers

If you chose **mostly a's**, turn to page 66.

If you chose **mostly b's**, turn to page 67.

If you chose **mostly c's**, turn to page 68.

If you chose **mostly d's**, turn to page 69.

You think the Popular Girl is cool.

Who she is: The Popular Girl is surrounded by friends, dresses with flair, and always knows just what to say. Everybody wants to be seen with her, waits for her to show up at school each day, and tries to copy her look. She wins the student-council election, eats at the most crowded table in the cafeteria, and gets attention all day long.

Why you look up to her: She walks with confidence and believes in herself. Everyone knows her name, and she always has someone to hang out with. She looks like she has it all, and you want to look like that, too.

What you can learn from her: You too can show the world that you're proud of yourself. Stand straight, smile, accept invitations, look people in the eye when you're having a conversation, get involved in clubs and on teams, and have faith in yourself.

She may be cool, but popularity doesn't equal perfection. Popular Girl has worries, too. She's just like you in a lot of ways, but she doesn't let insecure feelings stop her from trying new things that excite her. Some kids avoid her because they expect her to be stuck-up. She's also the subject of a lot of gossip simply because everybody knows who she is and watches what she does. For this reason, Popular Girl doesn't always like so much attention.

You think the Sporty Girl is cool.

Who she is: The Sporty Girl is strong and athletic. She is always picked first for teams, can be counted on to score points, and stays focused in a game. She goes after the ball with determination but also cheers on her teammates when it's their turn to shine.

Why you look up to her: Sporty Girl is active and healthy, and she makes exercise look like fun. Because she's in great shape, she moves with confidence and has good posture. As part of a team, she belongs to a group of girls who support and depend on one another. She plays competitively and shows what it's like to win graciously and lose gracefully.

What you can learn from her: You too can be fit, strong, and surrounded by people who encourage you to do your best—whether that means a team, your family, or a close group of friends. Even if you don't know anything about sports, you can start to be active by joining a beginners' group while you learn. Or when games break out during recess or after school, watch a few times to get the hang of it and then ask to play.

She may be cool, but it's not all fun. Sporty girl has to practice even in bad weather. She can exercise on her own, but when she's in the mood for competitive sports, she needs other people for a game. Sporty Girl has to lug around equipment and doesn't always get the position she wants. She also gets frustrated when she and her teammates don't play well and lose games.

You think the Smart Girl is cool.

Who she is: The Smart Girl knows the answers, aces tests, raises her hand to volunteer, and seems to do it all without effort. She loves to learn and makes homework and school projects seem enjoyable.

Why you look up to her: Smart Girl seems to know everything. She never gets embarrassed or says "I don't know" when the teacher calls on her. She's always leading study groups in the library, reading a book, or talking about something interesting she heard in the news. Classmates who need help call and e-mail her and know they can rely on her.

What you can learn from her: You too can move to the head of the class. Even if you've struggled with schoolwork in the past, you can take small steps to improve your grades. Add an extra 30 minutes of studying each day, read a book instead of watching TV, or take neater notes. Outside of school, get more curious about the world. Watch the news or use the Internet to find answers to questions you've always had, such as why the sky is blue or the earth is round.

She may be cool, but there's more to her life than straight As. Smart Girl puts a lot of pressure on herself and gets upset when she does poorly on a test. She may spend so much time studying that she misses out on other things. Sometimes she even stays up so late at night that she's tired the next day. She wants other kids to like her because she's nice, not just because she can help them study. And she hates being called a "bookworm" or "teacher's pet."

You think the Artsy Girl is cool.

Who she is: The Artsy Girl is creative. She has flair and style and comes up with new fashion ideas. Artsy Girl starts her own trends and can put colors together that might seem odd but look amazing. She isn't afraid of what people think. She is happiest when she is doing her art, whether it's painting, acting, dancing, singing, or playing an instrument.

Why you look up to her: Artsy Girl is not a follower; she has unusual interests and thinks innovatively. She doesn't mind when people look at her and isn't embarrassed by attention. Artsy Girl does more with music, art supplies, colors, and fashion than anyone you know. She has talent and creates unbelievable things.

What you can learn from her: You too can make a statement. Even if you've always been a little shy or try to blend in with the crowd, you can make small changes to get more attention. Get a new haircut, wear a color you've never tried, or take a class to learn a new hobby or make something you can wear. Just show your true self with confidence, and people will see your uniqueness shining through.

She may be cool, but being a trendsetter is a lot of work. Artsy Girl may inspire other people to dress like her, but since she always wants to be different, her look has to keep changing. And since her art skills aren't something she can use in every school subject, she doesn't always shine in the classroom. Instead she has to wait for art exhibits and school plays to show off her talents. Dancing, singing, playing an instrument, and being in a play all require her to spend many hours memorizing what she needs to know for a performance. With all that effort, she can feel let down once it's over.

now it's your turn to shine!

To you, the Popular Girl, Sporty Girl, Smart Girl, and Artsy Girl seem like stars, but you can shine just as brightly as they do. They have earned a reputation and stand out because of their talents. Now find out what makes you special.

Natural talent

Some people are born with natural skills or gifts. Maybe they possess a beautiful singing voice, the ability to memorize all kinds of facts in an instant, or the perfect feet for ballet. Think about a professional tennis player . . . it may seem as if she was born with a racket in her hands!

Extraordinary natural talents can lead to celebrity status, as they do for many famous professionals. But on a smaller scale, natural talents can help to set you apart. Are you good at walking on your hands? Can you say the alphabet backward really, really fast? Can you juggle five rubber balls at once? These are all talents that people love to see. Show one person, and you're bound to have a small crowd gather in no time. Get someone to take a picture of you in action, and submit it to the yearbook!

But don't stop there. You don't have to be known only as "the hand walker," "the alphabet girl," or "the juggler." Instead use those talents to continue building your self-esteem. The more often you prove to yourself that you can do something, the more your faith in yourself grows, giving you more courage to try new things. It just keeps spiraling upward until you're more confident than you ever were before.

Some things don't come naturally.

People who are good at things usually aren't just naturally talented. They have had to try something new, make mistakes, and practice—over and over again.

When you're first starting out, a new thing can be scary because you might have to take risks and be willing to be embarrassed. It might seem to take forever before you feel comfortable. It's that way for most people. Even your role models—no matter who they are—went through similar experiences. But your role models wanted to become the best they could be. They chose a goal and a place to start.

Reach for your dream!

If you want to feel more confident, choose a goal to reach for and take one step at a time toward it. The steps may be practicing, studying, or rehearsing. The work might not always be fun, and at times it will even be frustrating or boring. And it will take a lot of time. But if you keep at it, you'll feel more confident and become your own bright-shining star.

a good goal is . . .

your own.

Make sure your goal is something that you want to do—not something you're doing to go along with your friends.

something you can do SOON.

Instead of "grow my hair long," you might decide to "find three new styles for my hair while growing it out."

something to DO rather than something to STOP doing.

Instead of "stop gossiping," say, "I will stand up for people being bullied."

under your control.

If your goal is to get along well with your brother, remember that you can't control how he acts toward you. A goal you can control is, "I'll be nicer to my brother by playing catch with him."

very clear.

Make your goal clear using numbers or measurements, such as, "I will say only positive things about people for seven days."

step up your self-esteem

dos . . .

- **Use your potential**—everyone is born with some!

- Think of your self-image as a ball of clay, and **mold** it into what you want it to be.

- **Get through** a bad day the best way you can, no matter how long it seems to drag on. You will have a new chance to start over again the next morning.

- **Know that someone looks up to you**—even if that person has never told you so.

- **Make good decisions.** Use your common sense to decide if a new activity is good for you. Listen to your heart to tell you if it's something you really want. If it's right, make a plan and go for it!

- **Start small.** Choose a few short-term goals that are within your reach.

- **Try new things.** Even just attempting something you haven't done before will boost your confidence.

- **Practice, rehearse, and study.** Find something you like and stick with it.

- **Surround yourself** with friends who care about you and want you to do well.

- **Stand up** for friends and others who need your help.

- **Remember** that your friendship is appreciated.

- **Trust** yourself.

- **Train** your brain—nice messages only!

- **Picture yourself** as the success that you are.

and don'ts

- Don't let other people put you down.

- Don't call yourself bad names.

- Don't let your nerves stand in your way.

- Don't be convinced that someone else can do it better than you can.

- Don't be afraid to fail. Everyone gets a turn at it. Maybe today's not your best day, but tomorrow might be your day to shine.

- Don't assume that bad things happen only to you.

- Don't overreact. Little disappointments don't deserve big meltdowns.

- Don't assume that a little argument means a friendship is over.

- Don't believe that things will always be hard or bad.

- Don't settle for low goals. You can be what you want to be!

You can't control the world, but
you can control how you deal with it.
You can subtract the drama.
You can learn. You can be smart.
You can trust your confidence and your
common sense. You can take charge of
your own bad days.
Simply said—**you CAN!**

dealing with bad days

Everyone has bad days. Your day may feel depressing, embarrassing, or scary. Or you may simply feel crabby and tired. Bad days are no fun, but you can (and will!) get through them and feel better.

What is a bad day?

The problem with that question is that there is not one answer. Your bad day can look completely different from your best friend's bad day, your mom's bad day, or the president's bad day. No matter how you describe it, the events of the day have made you feel bad.

Out of your hands

Sometimes events that are out of your control can disappoint you or make you angry. A blizzard can ruin your outdoor ice-skating party. Getting the flu can mean no trip to Grandma's cabin this weekend. The bus breaking down can mean your field trip to the aquarium has to be postponed.

You can't predict when an ordinary day will take a bad turn, and you can't do a thing about it. Just accept it for what it is.

Just not quite right

Then there are the frustrating days. You wake up cranky for no particular reason. Your hair doesn't do what you want it to do. Your favorite jeans you planned to wear are in the wash. Your sister ate the last of the cereal for breakfast. You miss the bus. These things might make you want to scream, but they're not the end of the world. Having a meltdown won't fix anything and will only make you tired and late.

Move on

Whether the events of the day are out of your hands or just causing you frustration, don't let them eat you up inside. Instead, find something to look forward to in your day.

Take some "me time" to do something you really enjoy. Then have a private talk with yourself about how you would rank the bad part of the day on a scale of 1 to 10. If it's under 5, you can definitely get over it. Keeping to your regular routine will help you get back on track.

If your number is 6, 7, or 8, sit down and think about other things to help you feel better. Do you need a nap? A friend? A hug? A good cry? A snack? Help with something?

If your number is 9 or 10, you may need to find a shoulder to cry on because it may be a seriously bad day. This would be a good time to find an adult you trust to talk with. That person can comfort you and help you come up with a solution.

skyrocket your self-esteem

In a way, self-esteem is like riding a bicycle. When your self-esteem is high, the ride is smooth and easy. You feel as if you can pedal forever on the road to possibilities.

When your self-esteem is low, it's as if you went off the paved path and your tires got stuck in mud. It is hard to move and feels yucky and frustrating.

The good news is that **you don't have to feel stuck in the mud.** Even when you're not confident about something, you can still act as if you are. Pages 79–91 are filled with ideas to help you build your self-esteem. You only have to try one thing at a time to get started. Prove to yourself that you can do something so that you have the confidence to try another new thing. Take the first step now!

put your self-esteem on a fast track

Try: Doing a 5k run or walk for charity planned in your community

One of the best ways to make yourself feel good is to do something good for someone else. By participating in a run/walk, you will help a local organization raise money for a specific cause—supporting research to cure a disease, helping a town build a new library, or buying food to feed the hungry. You walk, they gain.

While you're helping to raise money for a good cause, you're also exercising. People usually feel more energetic and upbeat after exercising, which can be a big boost for self esteem.

You don't have to be super athletic to take part in a run/walk. The whole point is to give it a try and do the best you can. It doesn't matter if you even finish the race as long as you participate. Make the race more fun by entering with a friend, parent, brother, or sister. Or get a group together and wear matching colors and team T-shirts.

It's fun to be a part of something important and it shows you that you make a difference in the world. Charity races raise money for good causes and raise your activity level at the same time, which leads to a sense of well-being. It's a two-in-one bonus!

doing good for others is good for you

Try: Volunteering

There are so many ways you can lend a helping hand to people in need. Ask your parents to help you research a reliable charity. Then get to work giving back.

Donate money

- Give part of your allowance.
- If your community offers it, collect bottles and cans for recycling to turn into cash.
- If you're old enough to babysit, add a zero to your age and put aside that much money from each sitting job to donate. For example, if you're 9 years old, save 90 cents. If you're 12 years old, save $1.20. Once you reach a set goal, send in a donation.
- Start a bad-habit jar. Every time you do that bad habit, drop a dime into the jar to give to a food bank. By the time you have $4, your bad habit should almost be gone, and you'll have earned enough for a needy family to buy bread and eggs.

Other kinds of donations

- When your mom needs a minute to herself, offer to put together a jigsaw puzzle with your little sister.
- Visit a community center with a parent, and volunteer to help clean the yard and plant flowers.
- Make holiday ornaments to donate to residents at a senior center or as decorations at a hospital.
- Clean your room and bag up used books to donate to a library and old clothes to give to a charitable thrift shop.

You can feel proud when you give something away willingly and without being asked. And when you are proud of yourself, your self-esteem grows.

spotlight your self-confidence

Try: Putting on a mini performance

If you secretly wish you could be a performer but getting up in front of other people makes your insides feel jiggly, think small. The school talent show may not be in your league just yet (not that it can't be a goal to shoot for!), but you can be a star on a much smaller scale.

- Do a dramatic reading for your family. When your audience loves you no matter what you do, you're guaranteed a roomful of applause when you take your final bow.
- Sing karaoke at a family reunion. The words are given to you, so no memorizing!
- Play charades at your next family game night.
- Make your talent a gift. For your parents' wedding anniversary, make up a dance to their special song.
- Write words to a cheer or chant for the crowd to repeat at your brother's next football game.
- Memorize three new jokes to tell during dinner.

Whatever you choose, if you keep your act short, you'll be offstage in no time and prouder than ever for clearing another self-esteem hurdle!

speak up for self-esteem

Try: Giving a speech

Speaking in front of others, also known as public speaking, is the most common fear that people (even adults) have. So if the thought of speaking with everyone's eyes on you makes your palms sweat, your heart race, and butterflies circle your tummy at top speeds, congratulations! You're normal.

What's so scary?

If you fear public speaking, you can probably answer this question quite easily: forgetting your lines, losing your place, having your voice shake, pronouncing a word wrong, not being able to answer someone's question, not speaking loudly enough for everyone to hear, and so on. With all these things to think about, no wonder you're freaking out. The good news is that you can overcome all these worries with practice.

One step at a time

Instead of your first attempt being a speech about the periodic table of elements to an audience of hundreds, start small and work your way up. Think of it as a staircase to a bigger goal.

Step 1: Read a poem or short book out loud while sitting comfortably by yourself in your room. When that feels OK, take a step up.

Step 2: Read to yourself in front of a mirror. Make an effort to pause and look yourself in the eyes every once in a while. When that feels OK, take a step up.

Step 3: Set up your stuffed animals and read while standing in front of them. When that feels OK, take a step up.

Step 4: Read out loud to a family member while she's doing other things around the house. That way she's not concentrating fully on you. When that feels OK, take a step up.

Step 5: Read to a grandparent, aunt, or uncle on the phone. When that feels OK, take a step up.

Step 6: Ask a few family members to be an audience as you stand in front of them to read. Remember to pause at the commas, and speak more slowly than you think you have to. Lift your head and look out at your audience every few seconds. And keep breathing. When that feels OK, take a step up.

Step 7: Repeat Step 6, but with one or more close, supportive friends. When that feels OK, take a step up.

Step 8: Prepare a speech to give for a class presentation. Make sure you have a good understanding of the information; it's easier to talk about something you know a lot about. Repeat Steps 1 through 7 with your speech. When that feels OK, take a step up.

Step 9: You've done it! You're ready to give a speech in public. Way to go!

go solo to be strong

Try: Being OK by yourself

You're probably alone for small amounts of time throughout a day—while you're sleeping, bathing, and getting dressed—when you appreciate the privacy. But there are times you might feel as if you need another person around in order to feel "normal" doing something—eating lunch, riding on the bus, or walking in school hallways. Even spending time at home on the weekend instead of hanging out with a friend can feel like a downer.

Some girls enjoy spending time alone, while others dread it. The dread can come from thinking that doing something on your own draws more attention to you. You may think you look lonely because you *feel* lonely, but that doesn't have to be true.

Confident girls don't need to be surrounded by friends all the time. They like to be with their families sometimes, and they like to be alone sometimes. They don't assume that when a friend is out of touch, she is out of touch for good.

Go it alone

The point of learning to enjoy alone time isn't to spend all waking hours by yourself, but to be more comfortable with your own company. After all, when you're by yourself, you're the boss! Your brain needs time to sort things out, and it uses relaxing moments to do that. You find out about yourself—your thoughts, your opinions, and your dreams—when you take time to be alone.

show off your strength

Try: Teaching a skill to another person

If you have a special skill, such as yodeling, speaking a second language, knitting, making a digital video, or line dancing, it might be fun to share it. Also, teaching something to someone else reminds you of how much you know and makes you feel confident.

You don't have to be an expert to be able to teach something new to a friend or family member. You know lots of things that others don't. So why not share your knowledge?

Teach a friend to:
- shuffle cards in a cool way
- eat with chopsticks
- fold a cootie catcher
- do a French braid
- throw a football
- make a yummy snack

Teach a younger sibling or child to:
- whistle
- play hopscotch
- find books at the library
- count change
- tie her shoes
- knot a blown-up balloon

Teach a parent or grandparent:
- to fold an origami shape
- the words to your favorite song
- to play a board game
- a new joke
- to do a card trick

The more you know, the more you can teach. Keep learning and keep doing, and you'll keep improving!

give your self-esteem some star power

Try: Auditioning for a play or trying out for a team

Acting in a play or playing on a team takes guts. You will need to perform something that makes you nervous, all while being in the public view. And that's *if* you get accepted. When you try out, you might be rejected, since not everyone can make the team or be selected for a role in the play. But you never know until you try, so don't let rejection stop you from going after something you're really interested in.

Tips for trying out

Know. Find out the dates and times of auditions or tryouts. If you need forms signed, special equipment or costumes, or a physical, tell your parents in advance so that you aren't stressed by the rush of last-minute needs. Ask the audition or tryout coordinator questions if you don't understand something.

Prepare. Practice your lines for the part or your skills for the team. Look at how much time you have before the big day, and plan what you can do each day to make sure you're ready.

Buddy up. If you know someone else who is trying out, ask if she wants to pair up to practice together.

Rest. The night before the big day, get plenty of sleep. If you're nervous and can't drift off, focus on taking deep breaths and clearing your mind.

Try your best. If you've followed the steps above, you should be ready to give it your all. Find your courage.

Keep going. Mistakes happen to everyone, so don't get upset with yourself if you mess up on audition or tryout day. Just keep going as if the mistake never happened. Chances are, no one noticed except you.

Have fun. It doesn't really matter if you get the part or make the team as long as you had fun trying. If it's not fun, then it's probably not worth it. And if you don't get in this time, there will be other things to try in the future.

Start with a club

Clubs can be a nice way to meet other girls who share your interests without the focus on winning and losing. There are all kinds of clubs you can join:

• Girl Scouts
• 4-H
• Sports clubs
• Music, drama, and art clubs
• Religious clubs
• Academic clubs
• Hobby clubs

It's easier to join a club than a team because tryouts aren't typically required, and clubs usually don't have rules about how many kids can be in them or how you must perform. Plus, a club offers a great way to learn and develop skills in your area of interest, so if you ever want to audition or try out for something in the future, you'll be more prepared.

chat up your confidence

Try: Talking to a new person

Talking to someone you don't know well can be awkward. It can be hard to figure out what to say, especially if there isn't a conversation already going on. When you're with someone and feel as if you should be talking, it can be even harder. Next time the silence makes you feel a little tense, try some of these starters.

Are there any bands you like right now?

I'm trying to think of a food that begins with every letter of the alphabet, and I'm stuck on G. Can you think of anything?

I've had a song stuck in my head all morning. Does that ever happen to you?

I just opened a new pack of gum. Do you want a piece? It's strawberry—my fave! What flavors do you like?

I was thinking of trying to teach my pet a trick. What do you think he could learn to do?

Still nervous about getting a conversation started? Try practicing with your mom or dad first. Ask them to pretend that they don't know you and then try out a conversation starter. With their help, you'll be gabbing with new friends in no time.

mold your self-esteem into a masterpiece

Try: Being creative

You are uniquely you and no one else in the whole world is exactly like you. When you think about it, that's pretty cool. You have your own thoughts, your own ideas, and your own creativity. That means you can make something, and it will be different from anything else another person makes.

Celebrate your creativity and make something (or lots of things!) that represents just who you are. What anyone else thinks of it isn't important, because what you make will be your own true expression.

Not sure what to do? Here are some fun ideas!

- Write a poem.
- Draw a self-portrait.
- Play a song on a musical instrument.
- Write new lyrics to a popular song.
- Make a bracelet.
- Create a maze on paper.
- Draw your family as cartoon characters.
- Invent a new recipe.
- Act out a scene from your favorite movie.
- Decorate your school folders.
- Make a doll out of fabric scraps or yarn.
- Rearrange your room.
- Make an ornament or wind chime to hang in your window.
- Design a pretend theme-park ride.
- Take pictures of the plants in or outside your house.

help your self-confidence glow

Try: Being thankful

If you tend to think negative thoughts, your self-esteem will improve only if you make a shift to positive thoughts. But that's easier said than done. If you try to force yourself to think positive thoughts but come up short, then you may be overlooking some simple things, which gives those negative thoughts a chance to sneak back in. That's not a self-esteem circle you want to be stuck in.

A different way to think positively is to start a smile journal. Each day, write down at least five things that made you happy, such as:

- a funny joke you heard
- a cute puppy you saw on your way to school
- a friend who shared her cupcake with you
- a compliment you received for an art project
- something silly your little brother did
- a hug from your dad
- a rainbow you saw from your classroom window
- finishing a 212-page book—your longest yet!
- a just-because card in the mail from your grandma
- an A on your math quiz
- a new flower growing in your garden
- completing your homework during study hall
- your favorite meal for dinner

Keep up the journal every day, and you'll be looking for more reasons to smile just so you can write them down!

*Smile Journal

<u>8-23</u>
date

1. The afternoon pep rally.

2. Mom driving me to school instead of walking in the rain.

3. Pizza for lunch in the cafeteria.

4. Riley told me she liked the scarf I wore.

5. Grandma came over for dinner.

you can do it!

By now you know that the path to higher self-esteem starts with trying new things and setting goals. Track your progress by doing the following:

- Put a star next to the circles with tasks that you'd like to try.
- Put a circle around a goal that you're working toward.
- Write in the date when you've reached your goal.

Write a poem about my favorite things.
_____

Create a family cheer.
_____

Sketch a self-portrait.
_____

Learn a new dance style.
_____

Make a card for a family member.
_____

Try a new food.
_____

Do ten sit-ups in a row.
_____

Memorize the lyrics to a song I like.
_____

Stand up for someone being bullied.
_____

Make a gift for a friend.
_____

Jump rope for five minutes straight.
_____

Run for student council.
_____

Do ten push-ups in a row.
_____

Learn to ride
a bike.

_____

Learn five
yoga poses.

_____

Run a
mile.

_____

Read a
novel.

_____

Join a
sports team.

_____

Draw a
comic strip.

_____

Learn ten
words in a
foreign language.

_____

Perform
onstage.

_____

Sing in
front of a
crowd.

_____

Save
money for a
special item.

_____

Give a
speech.

_____

Try a new
recipe to serve
to my family.

_____

Start a
club.

_____

Don't see a specific goal listed that you really want to try?
Use these blank circles to set your own goals!

_____   _____   _____

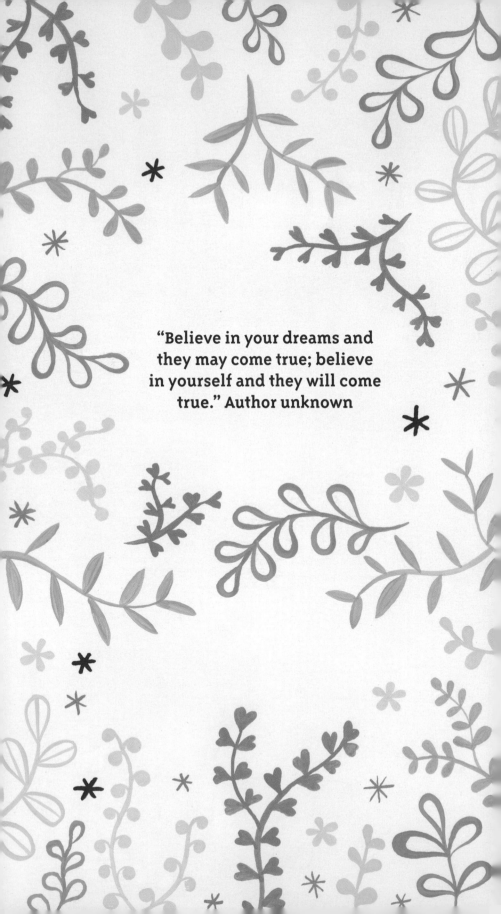

"Believe in your dreams and they may come true; believe in yourself and they will come true." Author unknown

Write to us!

At American Girl, we love hearing from girls just like you. Tell us what you think of *A Smart Girl's Guide to Liking Herself— Even on the Bad Days.*

Send your questions and ideas to:

Liking Herself Editor
American Girl
8400 Fairway Place
Middleton, WI 53562

All comments and suggestions received by American Girl may be used without compensation or acknowledgment. Sorry—photos can't be returned.

Here are some other American Girl books you might like:

Each sold separately. Find more books online at americangirl.com.

Parents, request a FREE catalog at **americangirl.com/catalog**.
Sign up at **americangirl.com/email** to receive the latest news and exclusive offers.